THE SIMPLY
SOLAR HOUSE

THE SIMPLY SOLAR HOUSE

GREEN BUILDING ON A BUDGET

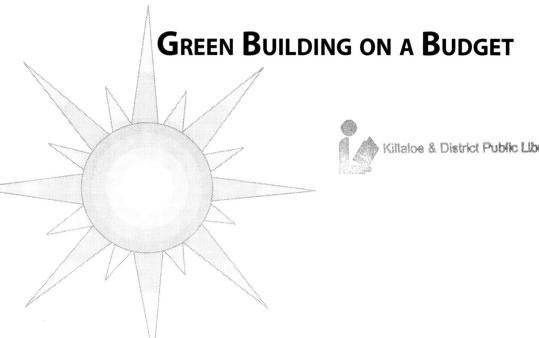

RICHARD & YOKO CRUME

Counterbalance Books
Duvall, Washington

Printed in the United States of America
ISBN: 978-0-9774906-9-1

Library of Congress Control Number: 2007932167

Dedicated to our parents, for their devotion to family
and encouragement to pursue life's dream

ACKNOWLEDGEMENTS

We are indebted to the North Carolina Solar Center for their thoughtful guidance and insight. Additionally, our project would not have succeeded without the expertise of our residential designer, James Morgan of Carrboro, North Carolina, and our builder, David Roberts of Bahama, North Carolina.

CONTENTS

PREFACE

AS MEMBERS OF THE BABY-BOOMER GENERATION planning for retirement in the not-too-distant future, we embarked upon a project to build a house that would be both comfortable and efficient for the two of us and our busy professional lives. With our only child away from home at college, we no longer needed as much living space as in the past. And with escalating energy, medical, and housing costs, we were determined to build a structure that would be economical to live in, especially in the future, on a retirement income.

We were also concerned about the trend in America to build larger, more energy demanding houses at a time when an increasing number of Americans are approaching retirement age. The costs to live in and maintain such structures are prohibitive for many retirees on fixed incomes, struggling just to cover doctor bills, pharmaceutical expenses, and other essential needs. Instead, the nation needs a new model for energy efficient home construction that is economical, aging-friendly, and respectful of the natural environment. This book provides the conceptual framework for such a house.

Our approach to home building is largely derived from our experience in researching, designing, and constructing a small, energy efficient, solar house located in a co-housing community in central North Carolina. Although our construction costs were no higher than other new residential construction in our area, our house consumes far less energy. The house was featured on the American Solar Energy Society's National Solar Tour and earned the highest rating for energy efficiency under the Energy Star® program of the U.S. Environmental Protection Agency (EPA).

We hope this book will inspire others to consider home design options with an aging America in mind.

Richard & Yoko Crume

GETTING STARTED

There are plenty of reasons to build an energy efficient house, yet most home builders do little to incorporate energy efficient features into their designs. Perhaps, skyrocketing energy prices and steadily rising utility bills are not strong enough incentives for many builders to deviate from the well established construction practices of the past. Also, many residential developers are held hostage to the common belief that energy conserving house designs cost more to build and, thus, are less attractive to buyers.

Imagine the global warming gas reductions if each of the million new homes built in the U.S. each year were designed to be more energy efficient.

It is true that many of the green home designs discussed in the popular literature can be expensive, sometimes requiring custom architectural plans, specialized construction expertise, and even exotic materials. It is equally true that a variety of highly effective energy conservation techniques is available to the average American home builder at little or no additional cost. When the resulting reductions in energy use are considered, it is hard to argue against including energy efficiency into every new home design.

Our house has monthly gas and electricity bills up to 75 percent below other new home construction in our area, yet cost less to build on a square foot basis. An added advantage of an energy efficient home like ours is that, by consuming less electricity, electric power plants do not have to work as hard, resulting in reduced air pollution emissions from many of these plants. When compared with a more traditional house not built to be energy efficient, our house causes about 14,000 fewer pounds of the air pollutant *carbon dioxide* to be emitted into the atmosphere from power plants. Carbon dioxide is the principal global warming gas that is contributing to our changing climate and warming of the planet.

The first step in building an energy efficient house is to find a plot of land. It is crucial that the land have good southern exposure so that the heat from the sun can warm the house during the cooler months of the year. For us, this

Energy conserving house designs make good economic sense. Not only are utility bills reduced, but a house's appraised value may go up as much as $20 for every dollar annual energy use is reduced.

was easy because our residential development requires building sites to be off-set from one another so that no house blocks the sunlight from another house. A wooded lot is also helpful because the trees serve as a windbreak from the cold winter winds while helping to shade the house during the summer months.

The next step is to find an architect or residential designer. While familiarity with solar and energy efficient house designing is helpful, we found that the most important quality is a willingness to explore various solar and energy conservation options and optimize them for the home owner's particular needs. We interviewed several architects/designers before making a final selection. By researching different house designs and having well thought-out ideas about what we wanted, we were able to more intelligently

> **SITING YOUR HOUSE**
>
> Orient the longest side of the house along an east-west line so that the long side faces within about 15 degrees of true south.
>
> This will optimize the amount of solar heating received by the south-facing windows.

We worked closely with the builder and an arborist to preserve as much natural landscaping as possible.

WHAT IS
UNIVERSAL DESIGN?

The concept of universal design involves making a home accessible, convenient, and safe for everyone, regardless of age and physical condition. As we grow older and begin to lose some of our agility and mobility, universal design becomes more important for many Americans. Some common features of universal design homes include no entry steps, one story living, wide doorways and hallways, non-slip surfaces, excellent lighting, and lever door handles.

Our approach to universal design was to include few interior doors, plenty of open space, electrical switch plates positioned lower on the wall, level hardwood floors throughout, levers in place of door knobs, and a circular floor plan for easy movement from room to room. Should negotiating the staircase ever become a problem in our two story house, we were careful to locate a bedroom/study and bath downstairs.

Everyone benefits from universal design. For example, no matter what your age, opening a lever door handle is easier than a knob when your arms are full of shopping bags. For many older adults, a universally designed home facilitates *aging in place*, meaning living in your own home as long as you can and want to.

quiz prospective architects/designers about their approach to our specific requirements.

Finally, we were ready to select a builder. Finding a builder with solar and energy efficiency experience is important, but finding one who is flexible and easy to work with proved to be much more valuable. For example, our builder was willing to spend considerable time investigating window designs and costs and discussing the exact placement of each of our 45 windows. To maximize solar heating during the winter months, we required that our windows be placed

Other builders had more solar and energy efficiency experience, but the builder we selected had the right combination of flexibility and patience to work with clients like us, who insisted on everything being just right.

a precise distance below the roof overhang and above the floor line. Many builders, no matter how good, would not have the patience to study these requirements and get the window placement perfect.

For us, designing a small, energy efficient house required considerable soul searching – were we willing to downsize and simplify, could we be content living in a small house on a small lot, and what would we do with all of the possessions we had collected over twenty-three years of marriage that we would no longer have room for? In other words, could we adapt to living in a small, five room, 1,600 square foot home when just several years earlier our previous house was a nine room, 3,400 square foot monolithic structure, and even then we sometimes felt cramped? Yet, this downsizing proved to be a blessing because, in simplifying our housing needs, we found that other aspects of our lives simplified too. Today, we are more aware of our impact on the environment than ever before and enjoy a healthier and happier outlook on life.

We also struggled with the question of what represents an aging-friendly design for new home construction. Certainly, accessibility, comfort, and convenience are key requirements for older, less-mobile adults. But we also wanted a design that works well for busy, mid-life, baby-boomer professionals with retirement still some years off. As we continue to age, our circumstances may change and an entirely new home design may be in order, one that meets our specific needs and circumstances at that time. However, the principles of economy and right-sizing, central to our current design, will always be relevant, no matter where life's journey leads us.

The U.S. has less than 5 percent of the world's population, but consumes about 25 percent of global energy production. Clearly, we can do better in improving the energy efficiency of our homes, businesses, and autos and eliminating energy waste. Residential housing alone represents over 20 percent of our nation's annual energy consumption.

HOME ENERGY CONSUMPTION

The most economical approach to designing an energy efficient house is to focus on those energy uses that consume the most power. On average, about 85 percent of home energy consumption is associated with just four uses:

- Space heating and cooling
- Hot water heating
- Large appliances (refrigerator, dishwasher, washer/dryer)
- Lighting

Space heating and cooling consume the greatest amount of home energy, representing almost half of total energy use (www.energystar.gov).

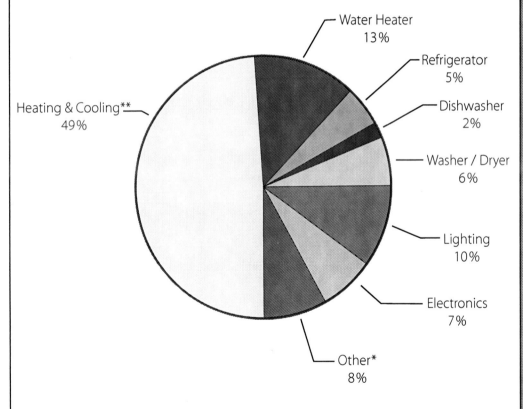

* Includes stoves, ovens, microwaves, and small appliances like coffee makers and dehumidifiers.

** Percentage will vary depending on location and climate.

ENERGY EFFICIENT HOMES HELP REDUCE GLOBAL WARMING GASES

Atmospheric concentrations of global warming gases like carbon dioxide (CO_2) continue to rise at a dramatic rate. This figure illustrates the longest available record of reliable atmospheric CO_2 concentration measurements (seasonally corrected), dating from 1958 (Mauna Loa Observatory, National Oceanic and Atmospheric Administration, Earth Systems Research Laboratory, www.esrl.noaa.gov). By consuming less electricity, energy efficient homes cause less CO_2 gas to be emitted into the atmosphere from coal-burning electric power plants. Coal combustion accounts for over half of U.S. electricity production and is a major contributor to CO_2 concentrations in the atmosphere.

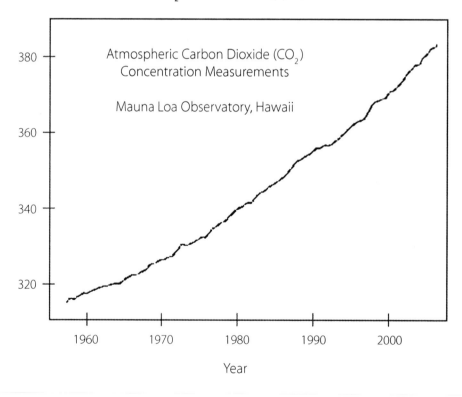

CO_2 Concentration (ppm)

Atmospheric Carbon Dioxide (CO_2)
Concentration Measurements

Mauna Loa Observatory, Hawaii

Year

ECONOMIES OF SCALE

*E*conomy of scale is an engineering concept meaning that the costs of individual units of production fall as overall production increases. In other words, the more of an item you make, the less expensive each individual item becomes. An automobile manufacturer finds that it is cheaper to produce a car when lots of them are in production at the same time. Similarly, an apartment unit in a building with other units is less expensive than a stand-alone house having the same living space.

Applying economy of scale logic to single-family home construction, a large house with multiple rooms should cost less to build per square foot of floor space than a smaller house, leading some to conclude that a larger house is a better investment. All things being equal, this logic holds true. Where the logic fails is that all things are usually not equal – larger houses often come with bigger lots and amenities such as two- or three-car garages, high-tech kitchens, luxury baths, and high-end appliances that may be absent from smaller homes. Also, large houses generally cost more to heat and cool, and maintenance costs are higher.

Smaller houses require less heating and air conditioning and fewer lights. And don't forget that your mortgage payment will be less too!

Larger houses are also a bigger burden to society. Because they consume more energy, large houses cause more greenhouse gases to be emitted into the atmosphere from the coal-fueled electric power plants that produce much of our nation's electricity. (Electricity produced at nuclear power plants does not generate air pollution, although the safe disposal of radioactive waste is a major environmental concern.) Also, the construction of larger houses uses more timber and other natural resources. A better approach for an aging America is to encourage the construction of smaller houses that cost less to build, are kinder to the environment, and are cheaper to live in.

In the past 30 years, the average size of a single family home in the U.S. has increased by over 50 percent.

While the average size of new, single family home construction is around 2,500 square feet, most American families can be comfortable living in substantially smaller homes. The following table illustrates the living space we believe most families can live comfortably in. Also, the table notes the energy potentially saved by living in a smaller house compared to the national new home average. These savings result solely from small houses having less interior volume to heat and cool, and substantially greater savings can be realized with energy efficient construction.

Decorative pillars, inoperable window shutters, brick façade, and a classy front door may add to a house's curb appeal but do nothing to improve comfort and economy.

FAMILY SIZE (number of persons)	LIVING SPACE (square feet)	HOUSEHOLD ENERGY SAVINGS (percent)
2	1,400 to 1,600	18 to 22
3	1,600 to 1,800	14 to 18
4	1,800 to 2,000	10 to 14
5	2,000 to 2,200	6 to 10
6	2,200 to 2,400	2 to 6

Of course, actual energy savings will depend upon many factors, such as the design of the house, use of energy saving appliances, and lifestyle of the inhabitants. But the trend is clear – the smaller the space we live in, the more energy we save.

Larger houses are often designed using a building block approach – rooms having specific functions are fit together into a floor plan where the occupants move from functional area to functional area. For example, in the evening after returning home from a long day at work or school, family members may first congregate in the kitchen, then move in succession to the dining room, living room, recreation room, study, and finally the bedroom (with occasional detours to the bathroom). This is a linear approach to home living that emulates the task-oriented, step-by-step way many of us do our daytime jobs. A primary consideration for the larger house's floor plan may simply be to ensure it fits within the house's exterior shell, often designed by developers to visually convey values of importance and success.

In a small, energy efficient house, the functional areas are usually more blurred. With fewer rooms, walls, and doors and more open space, the living area becomes multifunctional and adaptable – the kitchen may include a dining area, the living and recreation rooms may be the same, and a bedroom may double as a study. Because of the flexible use of space, living in a small house feels less constrained and more spontaneous.

People spend most of their time in just three rooms – the kitchen, living room, and bedroom. Design your small house around these spaces, making them comfortable, functional, and convenient. The other rooms in the house are less important … and may not even be needed.

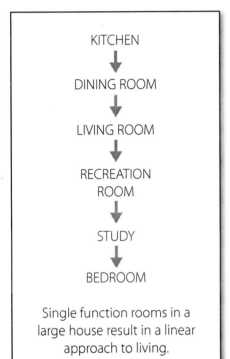

Single function rooms in a large house result in a linear approach to living.

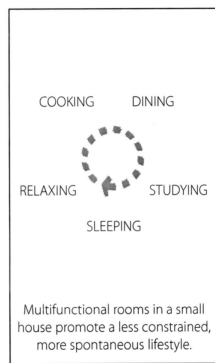

Multifunctional rooms in a small house promote a less constrained, more spontaneous lifestyle.

To live comfortably in a smaller house, the design must integrate light and space in such a way the house feels spacious and inviting. In designing our small house, the following guidelines were helpful in creating a design that is both efficient and comfortable to live in.

- Rooms that are not routinely used were eliminated from the floor plan, and multi-purpose rooms were included wherever possible.

Our use of multifunctional space includes incorporating the dining area into the kitchen, using the spare bedroom as a study when guests are not visiting, and locating the laundry area in a closet off the hallway between bedrooms. With doors on two sides, the second bathroom also serves as a hallway connecting two rooms.

- Spaces were sized large enough to be functional and comfortable, but no larger.

- Plenty of closet space was created to maximize our storage capacity. We included three walk-in closets and a large pantry — uncommon in a small house, but very important to livability.

- Long lines of sight and numerous large windows were incorporated into the design. The exception was the use of smaller windows in rooms on the house's north side to help insulate against the northerly winter winds and in bedrooms and baths for greater privacy. These smaller windows were placed at eye-level to provide a line of sight to the out-of-doors.

- The number of interior walls and doors was minimized, and open space was included in the design wherever possible. Where doors were needed for the bedrooms and baths, we used pocket doors. By sliding into the wall, pocket doors liberate adjacent wall space for furniture or pictures.

- The use of light wall colors throughout the house helps brighten the rooms and reduces the need for daytime lighting. Light colors also help distribute heat in the winter by reflecting sunlight entering the south-facing windows.

- Two decks and two screened-in porches were added to provide a visual transition to the outside and additional inexpensive living space for warm days.

- The need for storage was reduced by parting with many of our personal possessions, collected over the years, that were seldom used and of little sentimental value.

For us, the result of following these guidelines was a five room, 1,600 square foot house that is bright, cheerful, spacious, and highly functional.

A well designed small house is inherently aging friendly. Through its flexible floor plan, bright and cheerful spaces, low maintenance features, and reduced utility bills, it is much more adaptable to an aging society than its big house relative. By building our small house on a small lot in a community setting, it has been easier to develop lasting friendships, and we are comforted by the security of knowing a neighbor is nearby in case of an emergency – or just for a friendly visit.

Crume House Floor Plans

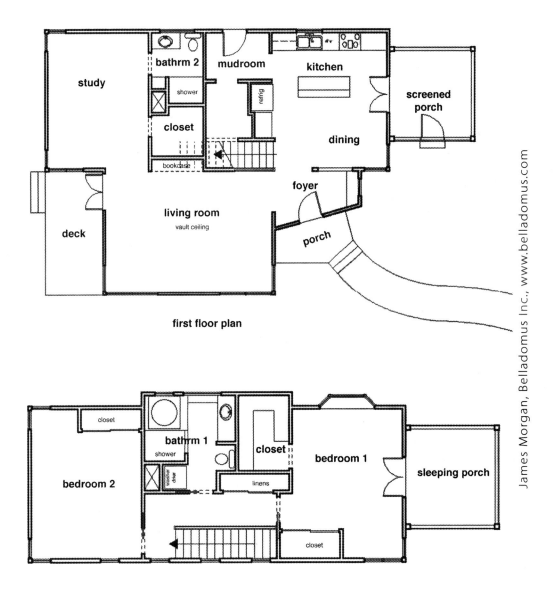

first floor plan

2nd floor plan

James Morgan, Belladomus Inc., www.belladomus.com

CRUME HOUSE HIGHLIGHTS

- 1,600-square-foot passive solar house designed for economy and energy efficiency

- South-facing windows have 30-inch roof overhangs for summer shading

- Solar water heater saves 75 percent of water-heating costs

- Utility bill savings are estimated at 50 to 75 percent

- Household energy savings reduce power plant CO_2 emissions by over 14,000 pounds annually

- $192,000 construction cost

- Construction completed January 2004

An open floor plan can help a small house feel larger.

First and second story screened-in porches add useful living space to a small house.

By sliding into the wall, pocket doors liberate adjacent wall space for furniture or pictures.

An outdoor workshop provides additional storage space.

OUR CHEAPEST ENERGY SOURCE

With the public's attention increasingly turning toward solar energy and energy efficiency, you would think that the use of solar designs and energy conserving technologies in new home construction would be more commonplace. While many new homes do include ceiling fans for cooling, insulating windows, and energy efficient appliances, numerous other techniques are overlooked. This is unfortunate because there are a number of solar and energy efficiency techniques that can be quite effective while costing relatively little.

By locating a stairwell in the center of the house, we provided a conduit for solar heating to rise to the second story. Diffuse sunlight also filters up the stairwell, helping to brighten the upstairs hallway.

We can think of several reasons why many new home builders are not fully embracing these techniques – traditional energy sources like electricity and natural gas are still quite affordable for most homeowners, high-tech solar applications may increase the price of a home, and some home buyers fear they may not be as comfortable in a solar house or that the resale value will suffer. Also, the traditional energy and building industries have powerful lobbies in Washington, and the federal government has been slow to enact strong solar and energy efficiency legislation.*

When it comes to investing money in something as important as a new house, it is understandable that people are cautious. But when critically examined, energy efficient designs can be highly effective, comfortable, and reasonably priced. Our home relies upon two low-cost solar concepts – passive solar space heating and solar hot water heating. For many homes, space heating and cooling and hot water heating account for over half of total home energy consumption.

Passive solar space heating is simply allowing sunlight to enter the house through south-facing windows during the colder months of the year. There are two basic types of passive solar heating – direct-gain and sun-tempered. Direct-gain designs incorporate dense, heat

---

*The Energy Policy Act of 2005, PL 109-58, represents a step in the right direction by providing tax incentives and loan guarantees for various types of energy production and conservation.

absorbing materials into areas of the house where they will be exposed to direct sunlight. Referred to as *solar mass*, these materials moderate indoor temperatures by absorbing heat from the sun during the day and slowly releasing it at night.

One popular approach for incorporating solar mass into a house design is to build the floors out of concrete. While industrial-sounding, colored concrete in a contemporary home can be attractive. Some house designs provide radiant heating in the winter by circulating hot water from a solar hot water heater through pipes in the concrete floor.

Sun-tempered passive solar designs are similar to direct-gain, but without the solar mass. Absent solar mass, sun-tempered designs can overheat if too much direct sunlight enters the house. For this reason, sun-tempered windows tend to be somewhat smaller than direct-gain windows, and temperature control can be a little more difficult.

Even if solar mass is in place, a passive solar house will overheat if the windows are too large, or it will not heat up enough if the windows are too small. The location of windows relative to the direct sunlight is also crucial. For these reasons, window size and placement need to be very carefully considered. Your state's solar center or energy office can provide expert guidance on window size and placement for your particular latitude and climate.

A critical component of any passive solar design is shading of the south-facing widows during the hot summer months. A common way to accomplish this is to allow the roof overhang to shade the windows. Because the sun is higher in the sky in the summer than in the winter, a properly sized roof overhang provides shading in the summer months, while allowing sunlight to strike the windows in

> For our house, there was little cost differential between concrete and hardwood floors. We elected to go with hardwood for the comfort of living on a wooden surface. Many passive solar house owners have made the opposite decision and are happy with their attractive and functional concrete floors.

SOLAR MASS

Solar mass helps prevent a house from overheating during daylight hours while keeping the house warm for a longer period of time after sunset.

Concrete, stone, brick, slate, and tile all make good solar mass. Even room furnishings like tables and chairs will absorb some solar energy, especially if placed in direct sunlight. Ideally, thermal mass should have a dark colored and rough surface.

the winter. To shade our windows, we designed our roof overhang to extend out about 2 ½ feet over the south-facing wall. However, these dimensions will vary from house to house according to the latitude, window size and placement, and climatic factors. (Several useful resources for window size and roof overhang are listed in the Appendix.)

Because our house is small and rectangular, every room has a south-facing window, and all rooms but one have windows on three sides.

WINDOW MEASUREMENTS

The window area through which sunlight passes is actually smaller than the window itself. This is because the window muntins, rails, and other framing pieces block some of the sunlight.

Assuming that the effective window area for passing sunlight is about 75 percent of the window size is a good approximation for calculations involving most types of windows. (For casement windows, the percentage is considerably higher.)

Other options for shading windows include awnings, trellises, and architectural roof-like extensions just above the windows. Solar screens (metal screening or fiberglass mesh that can block 60 to 80 percent of sunlight from passing through the windows), interior curtains, blinds, and insulated shades can also be very effective.

We allowed more east-facing windows because we enjoy the morning sunlight. Late afternoon sunlight on the western side of the house is hotter and less pleasant, so we installed fewer windows there.

Considerable sunlight can also enter the house through the east- and west-facing windows, and this can lead to overheating problems in the summer. Shading these windows is problematic because the early morning and late afternoon sun is so low in the sky that most exterior window shading is ineffective. (What works well on the south side of the house, where the sun is higher in the sky, does not work well on the east and west sides.) Consequently, passive solar homes often minimize the number of east- and west-facing windows.

Not all of the sunlight falling on a south-facing, vertical window comes directly from the sun. Depending on climate and location, as much as half is diffuse or reflected sunlight from outside objects and vegetation. This diffuse and reflected light can be blocked in the summer by indoor curtains, blinds, or shades.

Insulating blinds and curtains can also be useful in preventing heat from radiating through the windows to the outside during the nighttime, increasing overall solar performance by as much as 20 to 30 percent.

Another approach is to allow east- and west-facing windows, but to find other approaches for shading them from the low early-morning and late-afternoon sun. For our house, we enclosed several east-facing windows with two 10 by 10 foot screen porches, which help reduce the amount of direct sunlight entering the windows. On our west side, we built an eight foot pergola roof above the windows, which blocks much of the late afternoon sun while permitting some sunlight to filter through from the top. Other approaches include locating a carport or covered porch on the east and west sides. Interior curtains or blinds can also help block the sunlight.

When selecting windows, it is important to determine their insulating value. Modern, dual-pane, insulated windows can be highly effective in limiting wintertime heat loss from a warm room, but they can also reduce the amount of sunlight entering the room by as much as 25 percent. Many home builders are not concerned about this relatively small amount of sunlight blocked by the windows and opt for highly insulating windows throughout the house. Instead, we elected to install lower insulating value windows on the south side to ensure the full amount of passive solar heating. Elsewhere, we used the highest possible insulating value.

Aside from space heating and cooling, the next greatest use of household energy in a typical home is water heating, representing on average about 13 percent of total household energy consumption. Solar hot water systems reduce water heating costs by using heat from the sun to warm a heat transfer fluid that flows between a black box on the roof and heat transfer coils located in a hot water storage tank below. Heat is conducted from the hot fluid in the coils to the surrounding water, and then the fluid is pumped back up to the roof for another heating cycle.

> A typical American household uses 64 gallons of hot water per day!

Solar hot water heaters are quite effective and virtually maintenance free, providing 75 percent or more of a household's hot water needs. Backup gas or electric hot water heating is generally required only for those times when cold temperatures and cloudy skies limit solar hot water heating effectiveness. To further conserve energy, some solar hot water heaters come equipped with roof-mounted photovol-

We switch our back-up hot water heating element off for much of the year, attempting to live with 100 percent solar hot water heating. Realistically, there will always be a few cloudy, rainy days when the backup heating must be switched back on, even in the middle of the summer.

taic cells that generate enough electricity from sunlight to operate the heater's pump.

The payback period (amount of time required to recover investment through energy savings) for a solar hot water heater is often in the three- to five-year range, and the additional monthly finance cost on a typical home mortgage is more than offset from the very beginning by the hot water heating savings. Tax credits can make solar hot water heating an even better deal.

> **HEAT TRANSFER FLUID**
>
> Heat transfer fluid is simply a liquid that gets hot when warmed by the sun and then gives off its heat when circulated through tubing in a water tank. Usually, a fluid with a low freezing point like propylene glycol is used, similar to the antifreeze in an automobile's radiator.

Even the best solar house designs have limited effectiveness without excellent insulation in the walls, ceilings, attic, and floors or crawl space. By using six inch wall studs (a technique often referred to as value-engineered framing) rather than the more standard four inch lumber, more depth can be provided within exterior walls for even heavier insulation. Sealed crawl spaces are also highly effective in insulating floors and controlling humidity. A radiant barrier (basically, aluminum foil on a backing material) positioned near the attic roof helps prevent heat from radiating into the attic in the summer and radiating out of the attic in the winter. In warm climates, this simple and cost effective technology can reduce cooling costs by as much as 10 percent and heating costs by almost as much.

> **SEALED CRAWL SPACES**
>
> A sealed crawl space consists of insulation fastened to the sill plate and draped down the crawl space wall, overlapping a ground vapor barrier (typically, four to six mil polyethylene). No floor insulation should be used above the crawl space.

For homes constructed in colder climates, additional insulation may be called for. One option to consider is building the walls out of Structural Insulated Panels (SIPs). SIPs usually consist of two layers of wood sheathing laminated to a foam core, although other facing

With our relatively mild winters, we chose not to construct six inch walls. Because heat tends to move upward more than outward, we invested instead in extra attic insulation. Proponents of six inch walls argue that fewer wall studs are needed due to the added strength of the six inch lumber, thereby reducing the amount of wood required In construction by up to 25 percent.

materials such as metal, drywall, fiberboard, and plastic are sometimes used. The resulting product, having a cross-section resembling an I-beam, can carry structural loads in a home or can be used as cladding around frame construction. SIPs can be much stronger than traditional framing while providing superior insulating qualities. Although commonly used in wall construction, SIPs can also be used in floors, ceilings, and foundations. Other options for cold climate wall insulation include double masonry wall, straw bale, and cobb (clay/straw) construction.

In our community, well insulated homes that achieve high energy efficiency standards under the EPA's Energy Star® program receive a reduced rate from the local electric power company. To qualify for the program, the house must pass energy efficiency testing by a certified consultant. This testing includes placing a large blower fan in the front door, measuring pressure drop, and searching for air leakage.

> Furnaces are often twice as large as needed to meet a home's peak heating load. We were careful to buy only as much heating capacity as really needed to keep the house warm on the coldest night of the winter.

POTENTIAL AIR LEAKAGE POINTS

- Around windows and doors
- Wall electrical switch plates
- Where plumbing pipes pass through walls under kitchen and bathroom sinks
- Whole house fan housing
- Cold air return
- Attic door
- Electrical, plumbing, and light fixture penetrations between the ceiling and attic

Over 25 percent of a typical home's energy bill for heating and air conditioning can be wasted due to air leakage.

SOURCES OF GASES AND OTHER AIR CONTAMINTS WITHIN A HOUSE

- Gas appliances
- Pesticides and household cleaners
- Cats and dogs
- Off-gassing from carpets and paneling
- Paints, solvents, glues, and hobby materials

Our house passed the Energy Star® test with flying colors, although there were several unexpected air leakage points. While the areas one might expect to show some air leakage (around the doors and windows) were sealed tight, considerable leakage occurred through the wall electrical switch plates, where plumbing pipes pass through the walls under the kitchen and bathroom sinks, and around the attic-mounted whole house fan housing. These leakage points are easy to address, but we never would have known about them without the Energy Star® test program. If your energy efficient house is to function optimally, careful sealing of all potential air leakage points is essential.

While we may have convinced you to tightly seal all potential air leaks, some air leakage is actually necessary to maintain a healthy indoor environment. This is because gases and other air contaminants can build up to unhealthy levels inside a house, unless the indoor air is regularly replenished with outside air. However, if this replenishment occurs as a result of air infiltrating through leakage points, the result can be a buildup of moisture as the air follows a circuitous path around interior wall spaces and partitions, where mold growth can be a problem.

A better approach is to include a mechanical air dilution system that brings in outside air in a controlled fashion. This can be accomplished by simply placing a blower fan in an outside wall and opening windows on the other side of the house, although this is a somewhat energy inefficient solution that may be inadvisable on warm, humid days. A more effective solution is to incorporate a dilution system into the furnace and air conditioner ductwork that draws in outside air at a controlled rate every time the blower operates. By incorporating a damper into the outside air duct, just the right amount of dilution air can be introduced for the air exchange rate desired. Dilution systems are usually simple to install and add relatively little to the cost of a heating and air conditioning system.

For most of us, unless we live in a very warm climate, a back-up space heating system such as a high efficiency gas furnace will be needed on cold winter days and late evenings when the house begins to cool off. Other alternatives include radiant floor heating and ground source geothermal heat pumps. For smaller spaces, a gas or wood burning stove is also an option. (Wood stoves should be modern, low polluting designs certified by the EPA.)

EPA-certified wood stoves produce just 2 to 5 grams of smoke per hour, in contrast to older stoves that release 40 to 60 grams per hour (www.epa.gov/woodstoves).

*Rooftop solar hot water collectors are hardly visible
to anyone concerned about neighborhood aesthetics.*

Every room has at least one south-facing window for solar heating.

South-facing windows receive full sunlight at noon on December 21 (the longest day of winter).

Windows are fully shaded at noon on June 21 (the longest day of summer).

A pergola roof at the house's southwest corner provides shading from the harsh late-afternoon sun.

North- and west-side windows are minimized to help insulate against the cold winter winds.

A centrally located stairwell acts like a chimney by channeling solar heated air upstairs.

Two family members enjoy the warmth of a solar mass slate floor.

Recycled antique stained glass windows add charm to the house, but require careful sealing.

COOLING THE NATURAL WAY

Having a warm house with plentiful hot water courtesy of the sun is only half the battle. We also need a cool environment on those hot, sultry summer days that are becoming more common as our factories and automobiles discharge increasing amounts global warming gases into the atmosphere. Air conditioning is especially important as we age because our bodies become more susceptible to heat stress. Also, many older adults suffer from asthma, and for them, a cool, dry living environment is a necessity.

Depending on where you live, you may spend as much or more money on cooling as on heating. There are several low cost steps you can take to reduce your air conditioning bill or eliminate it all together. An important first step is to maximize natural ventilation. Providing that the outside humidity is not too high, a cool breeze drifting through the house can be more pleasant than air conditioning – and cost nothing.

High air flow/ low wattage ceiling fans are well worth the extra cost because they move the most air while consuming the least energy. Look for a fan that carries the Energy Star® label.

Where we live, prevailing winds are from the southwest for 10 out of 12 months of the year. Consequently, we installed casement windows that crank open to the southwest, thereby providing the best orientation for capturing the prevailing winds. To create a pathway for the breeze to flow through the house, we open windows and doors on the north and east sides. An open floor plan with few obstructions further facilitates the movement of fresh air throughout the house.

WHAT WE LIKE ABOUT CASEMENT WINDOWS

Casement windows crank open from either the left or the right. This flexibility is important when installing windows that you want to open in the direction of the prevailing winds.

These windows generally seal better than other window designs. Also, casement windows provide a wide open space for the sun to pass through, whereas double-hung and other types of windows may have muntins, rails, and other framing pieces that partially block the sunlight.

Casement windows have a free vent area of around 90 percent. This means that air can pass through 90 percent of the window without being obstructed by framing materials. This is considerably better than other common window designs.

What happens when the wind is not blowing? Nothing – unless you install an attic fan, as we did. Our large, 24 inch diameter fan sucks cool air into the house through open windows and discharges the warmer inside air through vents in the attic. It works so well that we can actually feel a breeze in the house when the fan runs, and usually only 10 to 15 minutes of operation is needed to cool down the entire house.

In addition to the attic fan, ceiling fans are also helpful in making the house feel cooler. On average, when in the vicinity of a ceiling fan, a person feels 3–4°F cooler when the fan is turned on. This means that you can decrease the air conditioning by 3–4°F, realizing a considerable savings in energy consumption.

The selection of the ceiling fan is important. Many of the less expensive models look nice but may be largely ineffective due to the absence of a good blade angle. Also, some fan motors run inefficiently, needlessly consuming extra energy. And sometimes the light mounted below a ceiling fan can consume even more energy than the fan itself. The best fan is one that has three or four aerodynamically angled blades (like airplane propellers), an Energy Star® certified motor, and energy efficient fluorescent lighting.

How you operate the fan is important too. The fan does no good if no one is nearby to benefit from the breeze it creates. Turn the fan off

> Because ceiling fans with lights cost little more than traditional ceiling light fixtures, you can afford to install a ceiling fan/light combination in every room.

WHY CEILING FANS WORK

Ceiling fans work based on the *wind chill effect*. Wind chill describes the temperature we feel on exposed skin due to the combination of air temperature and wind speed.

The breeze from a ceiling fan increases wind chill by causing moisture to evaporate more rapidly from the skin. Because evaporating moisture carries away body heat, we feel cooler.

Ceiling fans often consume no more than about 100 watts of electric power (the same as a 100 watt incandescent light bulb), whereas home air conditioning units can consume 2,000 to 5,000 watts. Obviously, ceiling fan use is more economical.

when not in the room, and don't forget to cut back on the air conditioning when the fan is in use. Many people forget this, resulting in greater overall energy consumption, not less.

Ceiling fans can also reduce your wintertime heating bill by helping to circulate the solar heating. To accomplish this, we run our living room fan in reverse in the winter, blowing the warm air upward towards the ceiling, where it disperses to other rooms and travels up the stairwell to the second story. For many homes, judicious ceiling fan use can reduce your air conditioning bill by as much as 40 percent and heating costs by up to 10 percent.

Natural ventilation is only effective when the air is relatively cool and dry. On hot, sticky summer days, there is no substitute for running the air conditioning system.

It is a common construction industry practice to oversize air conditioning units on the theory that a big unit will cool down the air faster. Also, many builders install two air conditioning units – one for the first story and another for the second story – so that greater control is maintained over temperatures throughout the house. However, from an energy conservation point of view, a better practice is to do just the opposite – install a single, slightly undersized air conditioning unit.

Comfort inside the home is determined not only by temperature, but also by relative humidity. If you have traveled through the Southwestern U.S., you probably noticed that high thermometer readings are much easier to bear than in other parts of the country. This is because the humidity in the Southwest is low, and this makes the air feel more comfortable. The same theory applies to life inside the home – if you can get the humidity down, the air temperature is less critical.

By installing a slightly undersized air conditioning unit, the unit will run a little longer and work harder to get the same temperature reduction as a larger unit. The secret is that by running longer, the smaller air conditioner removes more humidity than the larger unit.

With our slightly undersized A/C unit, we seldom have to set the thermostat below 80–85°F. Having low humidity in the house makes us feel healthier, discourages mold growth, and better protects our home furnishings.

And by removing humidity, the temperature does not have to be set as low to feel comfortable. Also, air conditioners run more efficiently when they run longer due to excess energy losses when they first start up. The result is that it is actually more economical to run a slightly undersized air conditioner than it is to operate larger unit.

An important advantage to reducing household relative humidity levels is that mold growth is suppressed. The ideal humidity for mold is in the range of 70 percent. In contrast, mold growth tends to be inhibited when home humidity is reduced to the 35 to 45 percent range. In our house, with our undersized air conditioning unit, it is common to see summertime humidity readings in this range and lower, even when the humidity outside is quite high.

Indoor humidity levels can also be too low. Below about 25 percent, human respiratory membranes dry out, infection defenses begin to fail, contact lenses feel uncomfortable, and static electricity becomes bothersome. In most areas of the country, indoor humidity levels this low are seldom a problem.

We thought that our shiny, galvanized metal (silver colored) roof would be ideal for reflecting the hot summer sun. However, we later learned that a white colored roof performs even better. Options include white enameled metal roofing, galvanized metal painted white, and other light colored roofing materials.

A final consideration in keeping the house cool is the type of roof, or more specifically, the roof color. The temperature on a black roof surface on a sunny day in the middle of the summer can exceed 170°F, whereas a highly reflective white roof surface may be less than 110°F. By having a light colored roof (white is the best), less heat is transferred into the attic and the rest of the house. This can have a dramatic effect on air conditioning bills.

Making smart decisions about cooling is important to an aging America facing ever-rising fuel prices and increasing global temperatures. Almost every year heat waves cause an increased number of hospital admissions and fatalities, mostly among older adults who are the most vulnerable to high temperatures and humidities. For some people, staying cool on a hot day can mean the difference between life and death.

*A screened-in porch off the master bedroom aids air circulation
without running the air conditioning.*

*To be useful, ceiling fans should be aerodynamically designed
and include energy efficient lighting.*

The house is designed to capture cool southwest summer breezes.

SAVING MORE BY USING LESS

By using less energy in the home, we save money that can be used for other necessities. Finding simple, low investment ways to conserve energy is a high priority for most of us, especially the millions of budget-minded, retired Americans and those planning to retire in the near future. One way to save on energy costs is to outfit the house with energy efficient appliances, lighting, and wall chargers.

Low energy consuming appliances may cost a little more, but the extra money you pay can be recovered by a reduced utility bill. This is especially true for energy efficient refrigerators, where electricity savings can add up to over $50 per year and the pay-back period may be as little as 1½ to 2 years.

The selection of appliances is a crucial step in building an energy efficient house. One sure way to identify an energy efficient appliance is to look for one with the Energy Star® label. The manufacturer's specifications are also useful in assessing the energy efficiency of an appliance compared with other models.

Buying an energy efficient refrigerator is particularly important because refrigerators consume considerable energy and represent a significant fraction of total household energy use. A low energy clothes dryer and high efficiency heating and air conditioning system are also necessities in a highly functioning, energy efficient house. Using a programmable thermostat can have a major impact on energy usage by cutting back on the heat or air conditioning when no one is at home.

Some appliances draw electric power even when not in use, adding a total of $10 or more to your monthly electric bill for a typical household. Examples include instant-on TVs, electronic equipment using remote controls, appliances with clocks, and cell phones and other electronics with wall chargers. There are two ways to avoid this non-productive energy loss – one is to be careful to buy appliances and electronics that do not draw electric power when not in use, and the other is simply unplugging the device when you are not using it.

YOU'LL GET A CHARGE OUT OF THIS

There are well over 200 million products with battery chargers in use in U.S. homes and businesses. Between 5 and 10 chargers are found in the typical household, and many consume energy even when not actively charging a product. Energy Star® rated chargers are a better idea, consuming on average about 35 percent less energy.

Electric lighting can also consume a substantial amount of energy in a home. Fluorescent bulbs are preferred because they consume 70 to 85 percent less energy than common incandescent bulbs, are relatively inexpensive, and last a long time. When deciding where to place fluorescent light fixtures, concentrate on those locations where lights are operated the longest – the kitchen, living room, and front and back porch. Lighting at these locations is turned on up to 3 hours a day on average, whereas lights in a bedroom or bathroom may be used much less.

Some people find the buzz from fluorescent light fixtures annoying. If this includes you, you will be happy to know that buzz-less fixtures are available at little additional cost.

DO YOU REALLY NEED A SECOND REFRIGERATOR?

A surprisingly large number of American households have a second refrigerator or freezer, or both. While undeniably convenient, these appliances can drive up your monthly utility bills. Unless really needed, avoid the temptation and try to get by on just one standard or small size, energy efficient model.

Compact fluorescent light bulbs are specifically designed to work in incandescent bulb fixtures. Typical wattages (a measure of electricity consumption) of incandescent bulbs and their compact fluorescent bulb replacements are illustrated below.

Incandescent bulb	Compact fluorescent
25 watts	7 watts
40	11
60	15
75	20
100	25

Even better than fluorescent lighting is no lighting at all. This can be accomplished during the day through the concept of *daylighting*, which simply means incorporating enough windows and skylights in your design to ensure that rooms are well lit throughout the daylight hours. Electric lighting will still be needed at night and on cloudy days, but by avoiding daytime use, your lighting bill will be substantially reduced.

Outfitting the interior of your house with energy efficient appliances and lighting, using day lighting, and avoiding energy-consuming wall chargers may be as important as the architectural design. Equally important is to modify your lifestyle at home to reduce unnecessary energy consumption. Many homebuilders with good intentions incorporate energy efficient features into their homes but do not pay attention to the little things we do inside the house to waste energy.

Modifying long-standing habits is not easy, but if every American homeowner followed these recommendations, the national energy savings would be substantial.

- When leaving a room, turn off the lights and ceiling fan.

- Cut back on the heating and air conditioning when not at home, and learn to live with the temperature a few degrees cooler in the winter and warmer in the summer. (A programmable thermostat with a 5°F setback can reduce heating and air conditioning bills by five to 10 percent.)

- Before switching on the air conditioning, try running the ceiling fans or opening the windows.

- Always wash the laundry in cold water, and use the clothes dryer sparingly (one large dryer load saves more energy than several smaller loads).

- Cook with the microwave whenever possible.

- Next time an incandescent light bulb burns out, replace it with a compact fluorescent bulb.

- Avoid leaving the refrigerator or freezer door open longer than necessary.

To provide adequate daytime lighting, our house design includes several windows in every room. Bathroom and bedroom windows were placed high on the wall, at eye-level, for greater privacy.

ARE SKYLIGHTS A WORTHWHILE INVESTMENT?

While skylights are relatively inexpensive and can really help brighten up an otherwise dark space, some caution is needed. One problem is that skylights can add unwanted summertime solar heating to a room because they are seldom shaded. Also, skylights are not always insulated as well as high quality windows, and radiant heat loss to the out-of-doors can be troublesome. As a consequence, undesirable heating and air conditioning loses and unwanted interior air currents can occur. (One skylight alternative is the light tube, which may have better insulating characteristics while providing almost as much light.)

- Always buy Energy Star® appliances.

- When not in use, unplug electronics and appliances having clocks and other features such as automatic-on that continuously draw electric current. (Alternatively, where a power strip is used, just switch it off.)

TESTING FOR ELECTRIC POWER USAGE

You can test a device's electric power consumption – both when and when not in use – by buying a kilowatt-hour meter. These low-cost meters are inserted between the wall outlet and the appliance electrical cord plug. By knowing the cost of electricity in your area, the appliance's electricity cost can be easily calculated.

A modern kitchen with energy efficient appliances does not have to be expensive.

Old fashioned metal ceiling tiles provide an inexpensive alternative to ceramic tile for the kitchen backsplash.

WHAT'S HAPPENING OUTSIDE?

The cost of most new homes includes landscaping – trees, shrubbery, a lawn, and architectural elements like trellises, walls, and statutes – strategically placed to give the house a pleasing appearance. Landscaping for an energy efficient house serves a different purpose – helping to cool the house in the summer while shielding the house from the cold winds of winter. Well placed trees and shrubs can reduce your air conditioning bill by 20 to 40 percent and also significantly lessen space heating costs.

We found that an old fashioned gravel driveway allows water to infiltrate into the ground, avoids runoff problems that sometimes occur with concrete, asphalt, and brick drives, and costs much less.

Deciduous (hardwood) trees on the south side of the house perform a very important function. By shading the house from the hot summer sun, these trees help keep the house cool. Also, the deciduous trees help cool the air in the vicinity of the house by transpirational cooling – basically, the cooling of nearby air as moisture evaporates from leaves.

Because deciduous trees drop their leaves in the winter, the sunlight is allowed to strike south-facing windows for passive solar heating. In contrast, coniferous (evergreen) trees, which keep their foliage throughout the year, should be removed from the south side. On other sides of the house, coniferous trees play an important role in preventing heat loss from the house by deflecting the cold winter winds. Also, trees on the house's east and west sides provide crucial summertime shading, which is otherwise difficult to achieve due to the low angle of the sun.

In deciding what to do about trees on your lot, a simple rule of thumb is to keep the hardwoods but remove any south-side evergreens. Remember to trim branches overhanging the roof to avoid damage

---

TREES IN YOUR YARD CAN SAVE YOU MONEY

Shade trees can substantially cut your air conditioning bill and, by blocking the winter wind, heating costs can be reduced too. An added advantage is that having large specimen trees on your lot can add 10 percent or more to your property value.

Our metal
roof, metal
clad windows,
and concrete
composite
exterior sid-
ing reduce
maintenance
costs, and by
eliminating
the front lawn,
we no longer
waste time
mowing.

from falling limbs during a storm. Also, if a tree is too close to the house, its roots can damage the foundation. Because deciduous trees will block some of the winter sunlight even after dropping their leaves, you do not want a forest outside your windows – a few well placed, mature trees will provide adequate shading.

HOW DOES EVAPOTRANSPIRATIONAL COOLING WORK?

Transpiration is the evaporation of water into the atmosphere from leaves and stems. As the water evaporates, heat is taken from the surrounding air, resulting in a cooling effect. Transpirational cooling in a forest can reduce the temperature by up to 10°F. So important is transpiration, that it accounts for about 10 percent of world-wide water evaporation.

Many energy efficient homebuilders avoid placing impervious surfaces such as paved driveways outside the house. Impervious surfaces prevent rainwater from naturally infiltrating into the soil and sometimes cause storm water runoff problems. Additionally, a natural surface like grass can be up to 10°F cooler in the summertime than asphalt or concrete, helping to keep the house exterior cool.

One exception to the avoidance of impervious surfaces is the placement of a solid surface on the ground in the immediate vicinity of passive solar windows. If the surface is light colored like a concrete pad, it will reflect heat from the sun into the windows and increase the solar radiation entering the house.

While not directly related to energy efficiency, the use of low maintenance materials is appealing to those of us with busy lives and limited budgets for ongoing repairs and maintenance. The low maintenance materials we used included a natural finish (silver colored) galvanized steel metal roof. These roofs are relatively low cost, require virtually no maintenance, and last almost forever. We also installed metal clad windows having a long-lasting baked enamel finish and concrete composite exterior siding that should outlast standard wood siding and require fewer paintings.

WHAT ABOUT A ZERO-MAINTENANCE LAWN?

As Americans get older, many of us are wary about spending too much of our precious time on lawn care – mowing, fertilizing, weeding, and reseeding. Also, the chemical fertilizers and herbicides used on lawns can be harmful to the environment.

Our approach to achieving a zero-maintenance lawn was simply to avoid having one. Instead, we worked closely with our builder to save every tree and bush possible, and any remaining bare spots were filled in with plants from our local nursery. (Plants native to your region of the country are best.) We also transplanted some shrubbery removed from the house foundation site.

Deciduous trees shade south-facing windows from the hot summer sun while allowing winter sunlight to shine through.

Rain barrels collect water from the roof gutters for landscape watering.

*A metal roof, concrete composite siding, and metal-clad windows
help make this a low maintenance house.*

Galvanized metal pipe makes a durable porch railing and never needs painting.

PUTTING IT ALL TOGETHER

As the population grows older and more and more of us reach retirement age, the availability of moderately priced, energy efficient housing has become a critical need. Relatively few new retirees can afford to maintain their previous lifestyle, especially given skyrocketing health care and energy costs. And baby boomers with retirement on the not too distant horizon are struggling to put away as much cash as possible into their retirement accounts. Everybody wants to save money and cut costs.

One way we can help make ends meet is to live in our homes as economically as possible. This means having an energy efficient design and conserving energy to the greatest possible extent. In many cases, conserving energy means little more than avoiding wasteful activities like leaving a refrigerator door open. In other cases, a little more sacrifice may be required, such as cutting back the heat a few degrees in the winter and wearing a sweater to stay warm.

We hope our small, energy efficient house will serve as a model for cost-conscious baby boomers and others seeking solutions to the continued growth of worldwide energy consumption and the potentially catastrophic consequences of global warming.

ANOTHER APPROACH TO CONSERVING ENERGY

Our neighbors, Carol and Chuck, are a retired couple who decided to conserve energy by building as small as possible. With three children grown up and living away from home with their own families, a big house was no longer needed.

Rather than incorporating guest bedrooms into their design for occasional visits from the kids, Carol and Chuck decided to always put them up in the local hotel, at a cost over time far less than building those extra bedrooms. Their 1,200 square foot house is all they need to live comfortably and economically.

Nancy and Phil, other neighbors with grown children, incorporated multi-functional rooms into their design that can be converted into bedrooms when the kids visit.

For homebuilders, there are a number of solar and energy efficient designs and technologies that can make a big difference in energy consumption costs. There are also alternative community models like co-housing that offer a blend of community support, economical lifestyle, and energy efficient housing. In our co-housing community, architectural codes mandate that the custom designed homes have solar energy features such as passive solar space heating or solar hot water heating.

When you are ready to design and build your energy efficient home, our best advice is simply to get out and talk with others in your community having first-hand experience with home construction and energy conservation. They can tell you what works and what does not and provide practical advice that you will never find in books. A good way to get to know these individuals is to attend solar energy house tours and join local clubs promoting energy conservation.

Because everyone's circumstances and needs are unique, the perfect house design does not exist. Therefore, don't be afraid to create your own unique design that addresses your specific needs and pushes your imagination to the limit. You will have fun in the process and may be surprised by your creativity and sense of purpose. By building a small, energy efficient house, you will save money, help protect the environment, and add your voice to a growing number of citizens seeking more appropriate housing alternatives for an aging America.

An aging America demands a new way of thinking about low cost, energy efficient, and environmentally friendly housing.

TEN ESSENTIALS FOR BUILDING AN ENERGY EFFICIENT HOUSE ON A BUDGET

1. Build small

2. Solar hot-water heating

3. South-facing windows

4. Extra insulation

5. Ceiling and whole-house fans

6. Natural ventilation

7. Thermal mass

8. Energy efficient lighting and appliances

9. Appropriate landscaping

10. Simplified lifesyle

Our first house, dating to before the Civil War, was completely uninsulated, including drafty single pane windows, five large fireplaces, and an open crawl space. (The wall plaster was held together with horse hair.) To its credit, the metal roof has lasted well over 100 years.

The new house is considerably smaller, well sealed and insulated, and surrounded by mature trees. It includes the latest energy efficient appliances and lighting…and, of course, a metal roof.

Our first house

The solar house

EPILOGUE

We have moved nine times over the past 26 years of marriage, including moving away from and back to the same house three times. Enough moving! When we built our energy efficient house, we resolved to stay put this time, at least until our retirement years. It did not work out that way.

Circumstances in life sometimes change unexpectedly, and after living in our new house for several years, we decided it was time to move back to our previous in-town neighborhood. There has always been considerable interest in our energy efficient house, so finding a buyer proved to be easy. In fact, we did not even have to advertise.

Several features of our house helped make a quick sale. First, there is a premium on energy efficient homes in most areas of the country, and our house was no exception. Not only do energy efficient homes sell at a higher price, they sell faster. When building the house, we were careful to eliminate unnecessary expenditures and concentrate only on the energy efficient and comfort aspects that mattered most. Also, we focused our energy efficient design toward techniques and technologies that have a reasonable cost and quick pay-back period. This allowed us to build the house for a cost comparable to the bank's initial appraised value and sell it several years later at a reasonable price for both the buyers and sellers.

Small, energy efficient homes help reduce the discharge of climate change gases to the atmosphere, a value increasingly important to potential buyers.

We have now embarked on a new journey – renovating an old house in desperate need of many upgrades and improvements. A number of lessons learned from building our energy efficient house are applicable to the old house. Leaky windows and doors have been replaced, south facing windows have sufficient shading, energy efficient lighting and appliances will be installed, and a solar hot water heater is in the works.

The Energy Star® program has investigated the most cost-effective improvements that can be made to an existing home to save energy, arriving at the following list:

- Sealing gaps, cracks, and other leaks (especially in the attic) that let in outside air.

- Adding insulation to the attic.

- Sealing and insulating air ducts in attics and crawlspaces.

- Repairing or replacing old or poorly functioning heating and cooling systems and appliances.

- Installing Energy Star® lighting.

Of course, the specific needs of a house will vary, depending on its age and condition. For our old house, we started by replacing the poorly insulated windows and doors with the latest, energy efficient models.

Bringing an old house up to a reasonable level of energy efficiency presents many challenges, but it also creates exciting opportunities to explore new materials and approaches. Also, we now have a better awareness about how bad habits like leaving lights on when exiting a room can have a big impact on energy consumption. And, we have rediscovered how an old house can sometimes have a charm irreproducible in new construction. As with the previous house … we are hoping to stay awhile.

A journey ends … and a new one begins.

APPENDIX

Why is energy efficiency key to addressing global climate change?

Our homes depend upon electric power, often generated by utility power plants fueled by coal and other fossil fuels. Because fuel combustion in power plants emits CO_2 and other pollutants known to be greenhouse gases, and because greenhouse gases are believed to cause warming of the earth's climate, much attention has been focused on these electric power generating facilities.

Climate change is a real and growing concern worldwide. According to the U.S. Environmental Protection Agency (www.epa.gov/climatechange), *"Scientists have observed that some changes are already occurring. Observed effects include sea level rise, shrinking glaciers, changes in the range and distribution of plants and animals, trees blooming earlier, lengthening of growing seasons, ice on rivers and lakes freezing later and breaking up earlier, and thawing of permafrost."*

While various techniques are under investigation for capturing CO_2 emissions, the most effective and least costly approach is simply to limit the amount of power we consume in our homes, offices, commercial facilities, and factories. Driving low-emission automobiles and cutting back on the miles driven can also make a big difference in reducing greenhouse gas emissions. Improving energy efficiency in our homes and elsewhere is essential if the climate change problem is to be mitigated.

U.S. Electric Power Generation

Other gases
0.4%

Other renewables
2.3%

Hydroelectric
6.5%

Other
0.1%

Nuclear
19.3%

Coal
49.7%

Natural gas
18.7%

Petroleum
3.0%

Electric power plants fueled by coal represent half of all electricity generated in the U.S.
(Energy Information Administration, www.eia.doe.gov/ fuelelectric.html)

Sources of Greenhouse Gas Emissions

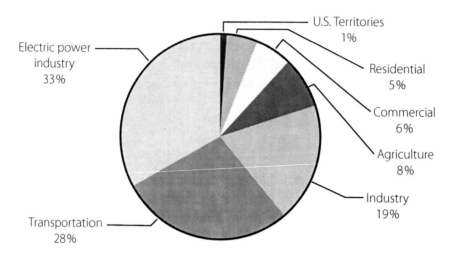

The electric power industry is responsible for one-third of all U.S. greenhouse gas emissions.
(U.S. Environmental Protection Agency, www.epa.gov/climatechange/emissions/usinventoryreport.html).

Resources

Much of what we learned about energy-efficient home construction came from simply talking with our residential designer and others who had been through the design and construction process. In this regard, the solar house tours offered every year through chapters of the American Solar Energy Society (www.ases.org) are a great way to learn from the experiences of like-minded homebuilders. Additionally, we found that the following resources provide very useful and timely information:

- Build It Solar (www.builditsolar.com)
- Efficient Windows Collaborative (www.efficientwindows.org/)
- Energy-10 (www.nrel.gov/buildings/energy10.html)
- Energy Star® Program (www.energystar.gov)
- Florida Solar Energy Center (www.fsec.ucf.edu/en/)
- Home Energy Efficient Design (www2.aud.ucla.edu/heed/)
- *Home Energy Magazine* (www.homeenergy.org)
- Home Energy Yardstick (www.energystar.gov/index.cfm?fuseaction=home_energy_yardstick.showStep2)
- North Carolina Solar Center (www.ncsc.ncsu.edu)
- *Solar Today Magazine* (www.solartoday.org)
- Sustainable by Design (http://susdesign.com/tools.php)

Energy efficient construction helps address the global climate change issue by reducing emissions to the atmosphere of greenhouse gases like CO_2. Excellent information on greenhouse gases and climate change can be found at the following U.S. Environmental Protection Agency (EPA) web sites:

- EPA Climate Change (www.epa.gov/climatechange)
- EPA Climate Change Kids (www.epa.gov/climatechange/kids)

Additional resources on climate change are available at the Climate web site of the National Oceanic and Atmospheric Administration (NOAA), the Climate Change site of the United Nations (UN), the Climate Change site of the UN Environmental Program (UNEP), and the Global Environmental Change site of the World Health Organization (WHO):

- NOAA Climate (www.noaa.gov/climate.html)
- UN Climate Change (www.un.org/issues/m-climat.html)
- UNEP Climate Change (http://climatechange.unep.net)
- WHO Global Environmental Change (www.who.int/globalchange/climate)

Printed in the United States
134122LV00004B/5/A

9 780977 490691